Stories for my Child

by *Samantha Hahn*

ABRAMS NOTERIE, NEW YORK

Section One:

Your Babyhood

WAITING FOR YOU

What I remember most about being pregnant with you:

_____

_____

_____

_____

_____

What I thought labor and delivery would be like, and how I prepared:

_____

_____

_____

_____

_____

Special events, trips, and things that I wanted to do before your birth:

_____

_____

_____

_____

_____

Other hopes, dreams, and imaginings:

_____

_____

_____

_____

_____

THE STORY OF YOUR BIRTH

Your due date:

_____

The date you actually arrived:

_____

What I remember most about labor and delivery:

_____

_____

_____

_____

_____

What it was like to see you for the first time:

_____

_____

_____

_____

_____

Other important details:

_____

_____

_____

_____

"I am here. I brought my whole self to you. I am your mother."

— MAYA ANGELOU

THE STORY OF YOUR NAME

Your full name is:

_____

How and why it was chosen for you:

_____

_____

_____

Other names we considered:

_____

_____

_____

Some of your nicknames:

"A few days after we came home from the hospital, I sent a letter to a friend, including a photo of my son and some first impressions of fatherhood. He responded, simply, 'Everything is possible again.'"

— JONATHAN SAFRAN FOER

BRINGING YOU HOME

My memories of our early days at home:

_____

_____

_____

_____

Important people who met you right away:

_____

_____

_____

_____

Special gifts waiting for you:

_____

_____

_____

_____

"Truly it is not easy to bring up a family," sighs Babar. *"But how nice the babies are! I wouldn't know how to get along without them any more."*
— JEAN DE BRUNHOFF

SATURDAYS WITH MY BABY

Here's how I would often spend a Saturday before you arrived:

_____

_____

_____

_____

Some amazing changes after you were born:

_____

_____

_____

_____

A few things that I missed:

_____

_____

_____

_____

BABY DAYS

Your general disposition as a baby, and the earliest signs of your personality:

_____

_____

_____

_____

_____

I was especially excited when you first learned how to:

_____

_____

_____

_____

_____

Things I loved best about your babyhood:

_____

_____

_____

_____

_____

_____

_____

_____

_____

_____

_____

_____

NEW MOTHERHOOD

Aspects of motherhood that were instinctual for me:

_____

_____

_____

_____

_____

Things I learned with practice:

_____

_____

_____

_____

_____

Advice I received (and from whom):

_____

_____

_____

_____

_____

_____

_____

_____

_____

_____

_____

STORIES FROM MY CHILDHOOD

A little bit about where I grew up and what my family was like:

_____

_____

_____

_____

_____

_____

_____

_____

_____

_____

_____

_____

_____

_____

A few wonderful things about my childhood that I've hoped to bring to yours:

_____

_____

_____

_____

_____

_____

_____

_____

_____

_____

MY PARENTS, YOUR GRANDPARENTS

My relationship with my parents when I was growing up:

_____

_____

_____

_____

_____

How that relationship changed when I left home:

_____

_____

_____

_____

_____

Ways that our relationship has evolved since I became a parent:

_____

_____

_____

_____

_____

How I feel when I see you with my parents:

_____

_____

_____

_____

_____

"We never know the love of a parent till we become parents ourselves."

— HENRY WARD BEECHER

Section Two:

Your Childhood

HAPPY BIRTHDAY

How we celebrated your first birthday:

_____

_____

_____

_____

_____

*Special ways we've celebrated
your birthday over the years:*

_____

_____

_____

_____

_____

_____

IN YOUR WORDS

Your very first word:

_____

Amazing things you've said over the years:

_____

_____

_____

_____

_____

_____

_____

_____

"What the child says, he has heard at home."

— AFRICAN PROVERB

OUR FAVORITE BOOKS

Your earliest favorites (the ones you wanted to hear over and over again):

_____

_____

_____

_____

_____

_____

_____

_____

_____

_____

_____

_____

Other books you've enjoyed over the years:

"That best academy, a mother's knee."
— JAMES RUSSELL LOWELL

EXPANDING YOUR WORLD

At an early age, you showed interest in:

_____

_____

I encouraged you by:

_____

_____

Our favorite places to play and explore:

_____

_____

Something I enjoyed teaching you:

_____

_____

Something you taught me:

_____

_____

OFF TO SCHOOL

When I first sent you off to school, I felt:

_____

_____

_____

_____

_____

Your own feelings about that day:

_____

_____

_____

_____

_____

How you evolved as a student (your favorite subjects, challenges, and learning style):

_____

_____

_____

_____

_____

_____

_____

_____

_____

_____

_____

_____

_____

"When I am not paying attention to my children, they appear to desperately need it. When I am giving them my full attention, they seem just as happy to play by themselves. It is as though they need to be certain of my attention in order to play their own games and ignore me."

— SARAH RUHL

SATURDAYS WITH MY CHILD

A typical weekend routine when you were about ____ years old:

_____

_____

_____

_____

Your friends:

_____

_____

_____

_____

Things we'd do as a family:

_____

_____

_____

_____

GOOD NIGHT, SLEEP TIGHT

Your feelings about bedtime as a child:

_____

_____

_____

_____

_____

Our nighttime rituals:

_____

_____

_____

_____

_____

What I'd do after you went to bed:

_____

_____

_____

_____

_____

MISSING YOU

*The first time we were apart for an extended period of time—how I felt
and what I missed most about you:*

_____

_____

_____

_____

_____

_____

_____

_____

_____

_____

"A mother's heart is always with her children."

— PROVERB

*"My mother had a good deal of trouble with me,
but I think she enjoyed it."*
— MARK TWAIN

A LITTLE TROUBLE

A time when you caused a bit of mischief:

_____

_____

_____

_____

_____

_____

_____

_____

_____

_____

_____

_____

_____

_____

_____

"Mother says as th' two worst things as can happen to a child is never to have his own way—or always to have it. She doesn't know which is th' worst."
— FRANCES HODGSON BURNETT

A LITTLE DISCIPLINE

Situation(s) where I had to say "no," and why:

_____

_____

_____

_____

_____

Situation(s) where I felt it was best to let you have your way, and why:

_____

_____

_____

_____

_____

"When your children arrive...your mind floods with oxygen. Your heart becomes a room with wide-open windows. You laugh hard every day."

— AMY POEHLER

A LOT OF LAUGHS

Times that you made me laugh (whether you meant to or not):

_____

_____

_____

_____

_____

_____

_____

_____

_____

_____

_____

_____

_____

WATCHING YOU GROW

One moment when it hit me that you were growing up:

_____

_____

_____

_____

_____

_____

_____

_____

_____

_____

_____

Toys and activities that you've loved—and some you've outgrown—over time:

_____

_____

_____

_____

_____

_____

_____

_____

_____

_____

_____

_____

_____

_____

_____

_____

_____

_____

_____

_____

YOUR BRAVEST MOMENTS

Some of your fears:

_____

_____

_____

_____

_____

How I helped you overcome them:

_____

_____

_____

_____

_____

An occasion when you were particularly brave:

_____

_____

_____

_____

_____

_____

_____

_____

_____

_____

_____

_____

_____

_____

MY PROUDEST MOMENTS

A day I felt so proud to be your mother:

_____

_____

_____

_____

_____

_____

_____

_____

_____

_____

"OH WHAT A POWER IS MOTHERHOOD"

— EURIPIDES

"The danger in motherhood. You relive your early self, through the eyes of your own mother."

— JOYCE CAROL OATES

DEFINITELY MINE

Aspects of your personality that you may have inherited from me:

_____

_____

_____

_____

_____

Ways in which we are quite different:

_____

_____

_____

_____

_____

MY CHALLENGES

For me, some of the hardest aspects of motherhood are:

_____

_____

_____

_____

_____

_____

_____

_____

"If evolution really works, how come mothers only have two hands?"

— MILTON BERLE

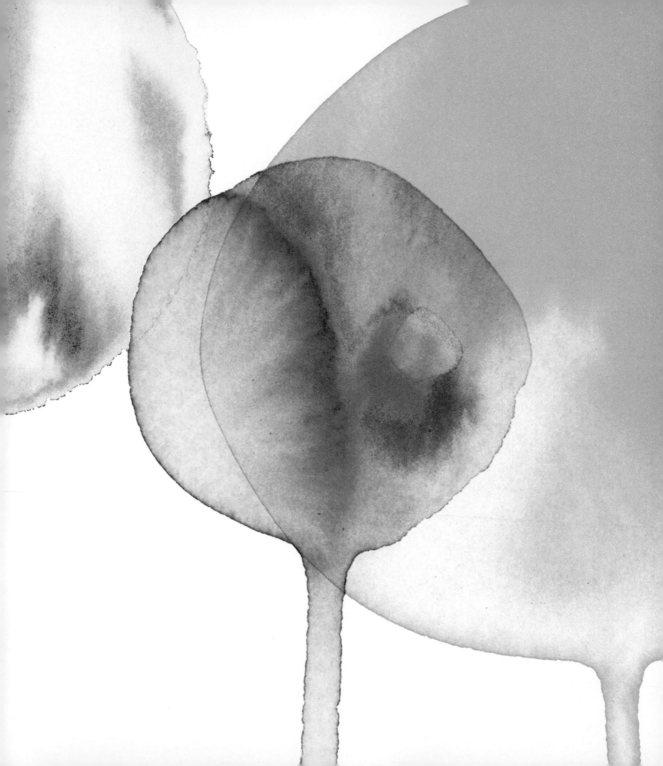

Section Three:

Later On...

Come back to this section later,
perhaps when your child is a teenager.

"The best way to keep children at home is to make the home atmosphere pleasant—and let the air out of the tires."

— DOROTHY PARKER

SATURDAYS WITH YOU

A typical weekend routine when you were about ____ years old:

_____

_____

_____

_____

Your friends:

_____

_____

_____

_____

A family ritual that kept us all sane:

_____

_____

_____

_____

"A wise parent humors the desire for independent action, so as to become the truest friend and advisor when his absolute rule shall cease."

— ELIZABETH GASKELL

YOUR INDEPENDENCE

Phases of your independence that made me proud and happy:

_____

_____

_____

_____

Things that I worried about the most:

_____

_____

_____

_____

Some things that I missed doing for you:

_____

_____

_____

_____

FAMILY ADVENTURES

One of my favorite memories of a vacation that we spent together:

_____

_____

_____

_____

_____

_____

_____

_____

_____

_____

_____

_____

"*I like to think of motherhood as a great big adventure. You set off on a journey, you don't really know how to navigate things, and you don't know exactly where you're going or how you're going to get there.*"

— CYNTHIA ROWLEY

THE JOURNEY OF MOTHERHOOD

Life lessons learned from being a mother:

_____

_____

_____

_____

_____

_____

_____

_____

_____

_____

_____

_____

_____

_____

LEAVING THE NEST

A letter with my dreams and hopes for your future.

Designer: Linsey Laidlaw

ISBN: 978-1-4197-1985-1

Copyright © 2016 Samantha Hahn

Printed and bound in China
10 9 8 7 6 5 4 3

Abrams Noterie products are available at special discounts when purchased in quantity for premiums and promotions as well as fundraising or educational use. Special editions can also be created to specification. For details, contact specialsales@abramsbooks.com or the address below.

ABRAMS The Art of Books
195 Broadway, New York, NY 10007
abramsbooks.com